MW00624357

THE

His Day of Delight

A BEKY Book ©

Jane Diffenderfer

This booklet is a BEKY Book publication:
Books Encouraging the Kingdom of Yeshua.
www.bekybooks.com

Cover design by Rubel Photography, Mt. Juliet, TN

DEDICATION

*This book is dedicated to my nine children,
Benjamin, Matthew, John, Sarah, Daniel, Luke,
Bethany, Aaron, and Joseph.*

"We are just seeds."

"Their descendants will be known among the nations, their off-
spring among the peoples; all who see them will acknowledge
that they are the seed ADONAI has blessed." (Isaiah 61:9)

CONTENTS

GLOSSARY

Hebrew words for Christians

Adonai - LORD

Challah - Braided Bread for the Sabbath

Echad - One

Elohim - God

Moedim - Appointed times with the LORD

Ruach HaKodesh - Holy Spirit

Shabbat/Shabbes - Sabbath

Shalom - Peace

Shaul - Paul

Tallit - Prayer Shawl

Teshuva - Repentance

Torah - Instructions of Moses

Yahweh - Name of the LORD

Yeshua - Jesus

INTRODUCTION

Our Heavenly Father created the Sabbath for mankind to be a day of delight full of peace and refreshment. It is a sacred time at the end of each week where His children are at liberty from the workday routine to slow down and rest. This time allows followers of Yeshua (Jesus) to concentrate on family unity, prayer, worship, Bible study, and fellowship with the Body of Messiah. It is an appointment with the King, a date with Adonai, and a rehearsal for the Messianic Age. Shabbat is a day that believers long for in anticipation of His Kingdom to Come, *Yom Shekulo Shabbat* – A time when all is Sabbath.

In today's frenetic world, Shabbat is the sacred time where mankind has the opportunity to commune with the Creator and listen to His instruction. Observing the Sabbath and keeping it holy are positive commands; one's attitude should reflect delight in the day. It is a command all mankind is invited to keep. Believers honor Shabbat not because they have to, but because of Messiah Yeshua, believers *want* to.

The motivation for honoring the Sabbath should be that of love, for the Father in heaven, His Messiah, and His children. There are bright promises for those who choose to honor the Sabbath as recorded by the prophet Isaiah:

> How **blessed** is the man who does this, And the son of man who takes hold of it; who keeps from profaning the Sabbath, and keeps his hand from doing any evil. (Is. 56:2 NASB)

> Also the **foreigners**, who join

9

themselves to the LORD, To minister to Him, and to **love the name of the LORD**, To be His servants, everyone, who keeps from profaning the Sabbath, And holds fast My covenant; Even those I will bring to My holy mountain, And make them **joyful** in My house of prayer. (Is. 56:6-7 NASB)

If because of the Sabbath, you turn your foot from doing your own pleasure on My holy day, and call the Sabbath a delight, the holy day of the LORD honorable, and shall honor it, desisting from your own ways, from seeking your own pleasure, And speaking your own word, then you will **take delight** in the LORD, And I will make you ride on the heights of the earth; And I will feed you with the heritage of Jacob your father, For the mouth of the LORD has spoken. (Is. 58:13-14 NASB)

Notice the above Scriptures say, "the" Sabbath. Sabbath is not about picking a day and choosing "a" Sabbath, but aligning ourselves with God's calendar and *His* weekly day of rest. The Sabbath was made for all mankind, Jew and non-Jew, male and female, to find the joy that only the LORD, Yahweh, can provide. The blessing and vision one receives in following His Divine instruction is life changing. The individual who takes the opportunity to observe the Sabbath enters into a slice of heaven on earth and finds the Sabbath rest in Messiah Yeshua.

1

BEFORE THE GIVING OF THE "LAW"

The Sabbath is introduced in Genesis when it states God created the heavens and the earth in six days, and on the seventh day He rested. God did not cease from creation because He was weary from creating the world, instead, it was His choice.

> Haven't you known, haven't you heard that the everlasting God, ADONAI, the Creator of the ends of the earth, does not grow tired or weary? His understanding cannot be fathomed. He invigorates the exhausted, He gives strength to the powerless. (Is.40:28-29 CJB)

The definition of the Sabbath, by Strong's Concordance (#7676) means: "intermission, repose, cease, celebrate, rest." When one makes the choice to follow Yeshua, who is One [Echad] with the Father, he or she finds that His Day of Rest invigorates and prepares the individual for the week ahead.

According to Scripture, God blessed the seventh

day and made it holy (Ge. 2:2-3). What God has called holy cannot be altered by the traditions of man. The entire creation revolves around the established order of the Creator's Sabbath day. The earth's twenty-four-hour rotation determines the day and night. The cycles of the moon determine the month.[1] The earth's revolution around the sun determines the length of the year.

Only the week has no sign in the heavens to determine its length. The seven-day week is defined only by the Word of God. The work week with its end at the Sabbath was established at creation. Everyone worldwide recognizes, whether it is understood or not, the Creator by keeping a seven-day week.

The seven-day week is not written in the expanse of the sky. It is not declared by the sun, moon, stars, or the earth's rotation, but by the Word of God. Therefore, in the absence of a visible, calculated reason for a seven-day week, it is the heavens declaring "the glory of God..." (Ps. 19:1). The Sabbath is His shining glory that is proclaimed throughout the whole earth. The entire population of the world witnesses the end of one week and the beginning of another, but does the world acknowledge the Creator by resting as He did?

1. See BEKY Booklet *The Biblical New Moon: A Beginner's Guide for Celebrating* by Kisha Gallagher for more specific information on the Biblical month and year.

After the creation week, the Sabbath is revealed again when the Hebrews traveled from the Red Sea to Mount Sinai. To provide the daily bread for the wandering Israelites, the LORD caused manna to rain down from heaven each morning. On the sixth day, the LORD told them to gather twice as much because the next day was the Sabbath, and He would not send any manna from heaven that day. (Ex. 16:4-30) This occurrence happened throughout the forty-year wilderness experience, and even before the "law" was given at Mount Sinai. Those who chose to do their own thing and seek manna on the Sabbath found out it was a rotten thing to do.

> **Those who chose to do their own thing and seek manna on the Sabbath found out it was a rotten thing to do.**

The Sabbath was instituted before the giving of the "law," also known as *Torah*, of Moses. The Sabbath is not a legal observance, but a natural occurrence designed by the Creator to reflect His glory. The Sabbath was established at the same time the sun, moon, and stars were created. Sabbath is part of the Creation order of God. Sabbath existed before the giving of the Torah to Moses and the Israelites. God's Word instructs:

> Remember the Sabbath day, to keep it holy. Six days shall you labor and do all your work; but the seventh day is a Sabbath of the LORD your God; in it you shall not do any work, you, or your son, or your daughter, your manservant, or your maidservant, or your cattle, or the stranger that is within your gates; for in six days the LORD made heaven

and earth, the sea and all that is in them, and rested on the seventh day, Therefore, the LORD blessed the Sabbath day, and hallowed it. (Ex. 20:8-11 KJV)

The work week of six days with a seventh day Sabbath is a weekly reminder that the LORD is the Creator of all life. One remembers the Sabbath to keep the focus on to Whom he or she belongs. "Know ye that the LORD, He is God, it is He that hath made us, and not we ourselves: we are His people..." (Ps. 100:3 KJV) Perhaps the Fourth Commandment begins with "Remember" because He knew we would forget. Every person needs to recall to his or her understanding the LORD's instruction, His Torah of Moses.

2

THE SIGN OF THE COVENANT

The Sabbath is a sign of covenantal love between God and His sanctified people. The passage in Exodus reveals:

> Speak thou also unto the children of Israel, saying, Verily my Sabbaths ye shall keep: for it *is* a sign between me and you throughout your generations; that *ye* may know that I *am* the LORD that doth sanctify you. Ye shall keep the Sabbath therefore; for it *is* holy unto you: every one that defiles it shall surely be put to death: for whosoever doeth *any* work therein, that soul shall be cut off from among his people. Six days may work be done; but in the seventh *is* the Sabbath of rest, holy to the LORD: whosoever doeth *any* work in the Sabbath day, he shall surely be put to death. Wherefore,

> the children of Israel shall keep the
> Sabbath, to observe the Sabbath
> throughout their generations, *for*
> a perpetual covenant. It *is* a sign
> between me and the children of
> Israel for ever: for *in* six days the
> LORD made heaven and earth, and
> on the seventh day he rested, and
> was refreshed. (Ex. 31:12-17 KJV)

This sign, the Sabbath, is to be kept throughout all generations of His covenanted people, Israel. His Spirit calls His children to be a holy, separated people, so that the world may distinguish between what pleases the Father in Heaven and what does not. This sign is to be kept forever throughout all ages as a perpetual witness for the generations to come that God is a covenant keeper. Forever means just that, *forever*. The Sabbath is a covenant reminder of the relationship God has with His children. He chose to rest on the Sabbath, and He has given His people the opportunity to join Him in that rest.

Honoring the Sabbath Day can be viewed as the diamond betrothal ring for the Bride of Messiah. It is a delight to be His, and keeping His set apart times (*Moedim* in Hebrew), is a sign on every Israelite's hand. The Creator rests on the Sabbath, and His Bride enters into that rest with Him. As she glances at the sign on her hand, she is passionately aware that she waiting for her covenant Bridegroom and King to carry her away.

> The ring is Shabbat! We are told in
> these verses that Shabbat is a sign...
> Just as the ring is an outward sign
> that the husband and wife belong
> to each other, so is Shabbat an
> outward sign for [Adonai] and Israel.
> It is an outward symbol that Israel
> and [Adonai] belong to each other.
> In a marriage, if the ring were to

be removed, people would have sufficient reason to question if the marriage was still intact. This is also the same for Shabbat. Since it is a sign that Elohim is Adonai Echad, removal of Shabbat from the midst of Israel would be like saying that the marriage between [Adonai] and Israel is over. Since [Adonai] promised in Jeremiah 31:35-37 [and] declares unequivocally that this relationship will not cease, then it would follow that the sign function for Shabbat is still in force for Israel. (Am Segulah, 2016)

In Leviticus 23, Yahweh told Moses that His holy feasts are His appointments with His people. The Sabbath is the first feast listed. It is a day of sacred assembly for the called-out of Yahweh to gather to read His Word, to worship, and to pray. The Hebrew word for this assembly is *miqra*, which comes from the root *qara*, and it can be translated as "rehearsal."

The Sabbath is a rehearsal of things to come in the prophetic future. Shabbat is celebrated in anticipation of the reign of King Yeshua, Who is Lord of the Sabbath. His return to Zion will be fulfilled with compassion, and it is an expression of His love for the bride. His rule as Sovereign, present on this earth, is earnestly desired by those who set apart the Sabbath Day to honor Him.

When the Bride of Messiah sets apart the Sabbath each week, she is demonstrating that she is ruled by the Spirit of her Messiah, and she is an active participant in the rehearsal of the Wedding Supper of the Lamb (Re 19:9). It is an intimate time for the *Ruach HaKodesh* (Holy Spirit) to flood her being. The mood of Shabbat is romantic, with candlelight, soft music, and fine foods. A table is set that is fit for the King in anticipation of His soon arrival.

Jewish tradition includes honoring the Shabbat as a Queen in which the Divine Presence, the Shekinah of the Holy Spirit, comes to rest on the home of those who observe the commandment. Songs and prayers for the Shabbat eve service include the concept of a Bride preparing for herself for Bridegroom.

> Come my beloved to welcome the bride, the presence of Shabbat we receive. "Observe and Remember" in one divine utterance, we heard from the One and Only God, the Lord is One and His name One, for renown, for splendor, and for praise. Come my beloved...Wake up, wake up! For your light has come, awaken, awaken, sing a song, for the glory of the Lord is revealed to you! Come my beloved...[2]

2. "L'Cha Doedee" from the *Messianic Shabbat Siddur,* by Jeremiah Greenberg

3

THE SABBATH BELONGS TO THE LORD

The Sabbath belongs to the God of Abraham, Isaac, and Jacob. While observed by a faithful Jewish remnant, the Sabbath does not belong to the Jewish people only, but to those who join in covenant with the Holy One of Israel.

In ancient times, during the post-exilic return to Jerusalem, in the days of Ezra and Nehemiah, the Jewish people fasted and prayed and confessed their sins and the wickedness of their fathers. They praised God for His glorious name and for creating the heavens and the earth. They remembered His faithfulness to Abraham and their forefathers. They praised God for the giving of the Torah. They were grateful for His laws that are just and right and His commands that are good. They praised Him for making known to them His holy Sabbath saying:

> You came down on Mount Sinai,
> and spoke to them from heaven.

19

> You gave them impartial ordinances,
> reliable instructions, and good
> decrees and commandments. You
> revealed Your holy Sabbath to them,
> and gave them commandments,
> statutes, and a law through Your
> servant Moses. (Ne. 9:13-14 HCSB)

Believers in Messiah Yeshua also can be delighted that He has made His holy Sabbath Day known. It is Divine revelation of the Spirit of God that convicts the heart of sin. When the conviction that one has not heeded the instructions of His Torah settles in the soul, repentance can follow. It is a wonderful thing to be convicted by His Spirit to obey His commandments. Some will still contend that the Sabbath is only for Israel. Is that really what the Bible teaches? The prophet Isaiah reveals that the Sabbath is not only for the Jewish people, but also for the nations.

> Thus saith the LORD, Keep ye
> judgment, and do justice: for my
> salvation *is* near to come, and
> my righteousness to be revealed.
> Blessed *is* the man *that* doeth this,
> and the son of man *that* layeth hold
> on it; that keepeth the Sabbath from
> polluting it, and keepeth his hand
> from doing any evil. (Is. 56:1-2 KJV)

> Neither let the son of the stranger,
> that hath joined himself to the LORD,
> speak, saying, The LORD hath utterly
> separated me from his people:
> neither let the eunuch say, Behold, I
> *am* a dry tree. (Is. 56:3 KJV)

> For thus saith the LORD unto the
> eunuchs that keep my Sabbaths,
> and choose *the things* that please
> me, and take hold of my covenant;
> Even unto them will I give in mine

house and within my walls a place
and a name better than of sons
and of daughters: I will give them an
everlasting name, that shall not be
cut off. (Is. 56:4-5 KJV)

Also the sons of the stranger, that
join themselves to the LORD, to
serve him, and to love the name of
the LORD, to be his servants, every
one that keepeth the Sabbath from
polluting it, and taketh hold of my
covenant; Even them will I bring to
my holy mountain, and make them
joyful in my house of prayer: their
burnt offerings and their sacrifices
shall be accepted upon mine altar;
for mine house shall be called an
house of prayer for all people. (Is.
56:6-7 KJV)

Everyone includes everyone! All who take hold of
the new covenant in Messiah Yeshua are free to
take hold of the blessing of the Sabbath Day. All
mankind may keep the Sabbath as a sign of being
in covenant with the God of Abraham, Isaac, and
Jacob. In Messiah, we are Abraham's seed and heirs
according to the promise. (Ga. 3:29)

Everyone includes everyone!

4

THE DAY IN WHICH TO DELIGHT

The Sabbath was created for Divine delight, a time when God and man are Echad. Prophets are continually speaking truth to return the Bride of God back to her marriage vows, back to the covenant. The Prophet Isaiah continues to preach another promise regarding the Sabbath:

> If you keep from desecrating the Sabbath, from doing whatever you want on My holy day; if you call the Sabbath a delight, and the holy day of the LORD honorable; if you honor it, not going your own ways, seeking your own pleasure, or talking too much; then you will delight yourself in the LORD, and I will make you ride over the heights of the land, and let you enjoy the heritage of your father Jacob." For the mouth of the LORD has spoken. (Is. 58: 13-14 HCSB)

There are "if-then" promises in God's Word. Go back and re-read the above. Circle how many times the word "if" is included in this passage. It is every person's choice of how he or she chooses to obey His Word. Free will is a choice. "If you keep," "if you call," and "if you honor," is followed by the "then you will." When all of the above conditions are answered with a resounding "yes," *then* a believer will experience the promise of delighting himself in the LORD.

The Hebrew word for delight in regard to the Sabbath indicates softness toward God, which allows one to be delicately pampered by the LORD. Congregations that host Shabbat gatherings often have a simple festive meal of refreshments that is called *oneg*, the Hebrew word that means delight. Dainties, delicate foods, and delicious treats are served to those who gather for oneg.

Sometimes believers desire the blessing without keeping the requirements of the blessing. Conditional promises are based on keeping the conditions of the promise. In a covenant, one can't have the *blessing* of obedience without the *actions* of obedience.

Part of the option of being blessed is choosing to do His will, not one's own. If a disciple of Yeshua calls the Sabbath a delight, he or she is agreeing with the LORD. If a person calls it a burden, something that is done away with, or no longer relevant, then one agrees with the forces of darkness that oppose Messiah Yeshua, a force also known as the anti-messiah.

There is a man of lawlessness that opposes the Torah of Messiah, and the New Covenant Scriptures warn us to be on watch.

> Don't let anyone deceive you in
> any way. For the Day will not come
> until after the Apostasy has come
> and the man who separates himself
> from *Torah* has been revealed,
> the one destined for doom. He
> will oppose himself to everything

that people call a god or make an object of worship; he will put himself above them all... (2 Th. 2:3-4 CJB)

No child of God should want to align his or her life with the one who separates himself from the instructions of Adonai. Our God promised the blessing to Father Abraham and that promise included descendants who would inherit the Land of Israel. Which one of us would not want to ride on the heights of His promise? Who would not want to share in the heritage, the inheritance of the land of Jacob?

It is a choice mankind is freely offered, an if-then choice. Every day we choose whom we will serve. Are we doing our own pleasure, or Adonai's?

> *If you call the Sabbath a delight.*
> Shabbat is a weekly dress rehearsal for the Messianic Age, and intimation of paradise regained, when all hierarchies of wealth, power and status are suspended, and master and servant enjoy the same freedom. One day in seven we cease to be creators and celebrate our "createdness," catching a glimpse of the harmony of the universe – the creative Unity at the heart of created diversity – and in the silence of the soul hear the song of the earth and the music of the heavens. (Sacks, 2008)

The above glimpse of Shabbat was taken from an Orthodox Jewish prayer book for Yom Kippur. It is interesting how Messianic keeping the Sabbath is! The revelation of Messiah is displayed by honoring the Kingdom of Elohim, the Creator and Sustainer of all life, when we rest with Him.

5

WHAT DO THE TEN COMMANDMENTS SAY?

Believers in Messiah claim that they stand on the firm foundation of the Ten Commandments, but do they? What do the commandments really say versus what we have heard they say?

> Then God spoke all these words, saying,
>
> 1) "I am the LORD your God, who brought you out of the land of Egypt, out of the house of slavery. You shall have no other gods before Me."
>
> 2) You shall not make for yourself an idol, or any likeness of what is in heaven above or on the earth beneath or in the water under the earth. You shall not worship them or serve them; for I, the LORD your God, am a jealous God, visiting the iniquity of the fathers on the children, on the third and the fourth generations of those who hate Me, but showing

lovingkindness to thousands, to those who love Me and keep My commandments.

3) You shall not take the name of the LORD your God in vain, for the LORD will not leave him unpunished who takes His name in vain.

4) Remember the Sabbath day, to keep it holy. Six days you shall labor and do all your work, but the seventh day is a Sabbath of the LORD your God; *in it* you shall not do any work, you or your son or your daughter, your male or your female servant or your cattle or your sojourner who stays with you. For in six days the LORD made the heavens and the earth, the sea and all that is in them, and rested on the seventh day; therefore the LORD blessed the Sabbath day and made it holy.

5) Honor your father and your mother, that your days may be prolonged in the land which the LORD your God gives you.

6) You shall not murder.

7) You shall not commit adultery.

8) You shall not steal.

9) You shall not bear false witness against your neighbor.

10) You shall not covet your neighbor's house; you shall not covet your neighbor's wife or his male servant or his female servant or

his ox or his donkey or anything that belongs to your neighbor. (Ex. 20:1-17 NASB)

There are many professing Christians who believe the Torah of Moses has been rescinded for the disciples of Messiah. It is a tragic mistake, birthed by an anti-Semitic, anti-Jewish spirit that has invaded the church. It is as though when God said "forever" (Ex. 31:17) about the Sabbath, He really didn't mean it.

This spirit of lawlessness tells believers that the "freedom in Christ" is freedom *from* the commandments of God. Yeshua did not set His people free to be disobedient. He set them free from the bondage of sin and death, not the Torah of God. The truth is that all Scripture is given for instruction in righteousness, including the Torah (2 Ti. 3:16). All the Ten Commandments, the great summary of how to love Adonai and one's neighbor, applies to all believers in Messiah Yeshua.

No one who trusts in Yeshua as Savior would suggest that a holy people are free from laws like, "You shall not murder," "You shall not commit adultery," or "You shall not steal." So why does the modern church state that we are free from the fourth commandment, "Remember the Sabbath day to keep it holy?" If the sixth, seventh, and eighth commandments are still valid, is not the fourth one also?

> All scripture *is* given by inspiration of God, and *is* profitable for doctrine, for reproof, for correction, for instruction in righteousness: That the man of God may be perfect, thoroughly furnished unto all good works. (2 Ti. 3:16-17 KJV)

Keeping the Sabbath holy is one of the good works with which we are to be thoroughly furnished and perfected to do! According to all Scripture, the

Torah of Moses included, Sabbath is a good thing for disciples of Yeshua to do.

Some Christians will champion that they keep the "moral" law, and therefore, exclude the Sabbath as though it is not part of the moral code of God. All the commandments of God, including those pertaining to the Sabbath, are moral. As the Apostle Paul wrote: "Wherefore the law *is* holy, and the commandment holy, and just, and good." (Ro. 7:12) Human minds cannot justify doing away with what is holy just because it is inconvenient.

If one's ears itch to hear teachings that are contrary to the written instructions of God, it is necessary to check with the Holy Spirit to see if one is being led into all truth or in a different direction. It is possible to be deceived by another "Christ," to discern truth from error remember the Sprit and the Word are in agreement. The Spirit of the law, the teaching and instruction of Torah, upholds the commandments of God.

6

THE SAME YESTERDAY, TODAY, AND FOREVER

Many church leaders teach that Christians are not under the laws of the Old Covenant; the Church is now under grace. The theory is that under the Old Covenant, God dealt harshly with His people, and now He deals more kindly with His creation. Many churches teach that the Church is now in the "dispensation of grace" under the New Covenant, and the LORD is now merciful to His people. This theory is contrary to Scripture; God says, "I am the LORD, I change not." (Ma. 3:6) Adonai has always been merciful to His children. He has always been willing to forgive the repentant. He is the same yesterday, today, and forever (He. 13:18).

Mercy and truth, grace and Torah, are two sides of the same coin. One cannot experience grace without God's Torah. One cannot know mercy apart from the truth of His Word. Psalm 119 informs that grace and law are not opposing concepts, but two compatible expressions of faith. One does not exist without the other. Grace actually comes through God's instructions for His people.

> Keep me from deceitful ways: **be gracious** to me **through your law** [Torah]...I run in the path of your commands, for you have set my heart free. (Ps. 119:29-32 NIV)

There are a couple Hebrew words for mercy translated into English versions of the Bible. The most commonly known one is *chesed*, often translated as "lovingkindness." It is an attribute of God, His character that endures forever, and his character does not change.

> But the mercy (chesed) of the LORD *is* from everlasting to everlasting upon them that fear Him, and His righteousness unto children's children; to such as keep His covenant, and to those that remember His commandments to do them. (Ps. 103:17-18 NASB)

Chesed is dependent upon an established relationship; it involves a bond between the parties involved. One may have grace (*chen* in Hebrew) as an expression of pity for a homeless stranger. But chesed is different; it involves a relationship that continues throughout time. Dr. Skip Moen puts it this way:

> To children's children – What's the connection? *Hesed* operates between related parties. It isn't like grace (*hen*). *Hesed* presupposes some already-existing connection. Once in place, *hesed* governs the continuing relationship between the parties—and the extension of that bonded relationship to generations. (Moen, 2015)

Chesed, Yahweh's mercy, is available to all who

choose to keep His covenant and obey His Word. Here are just a few examples of how chesed is translated into the various English versions of the Bible in Ps. 25:10:

> All ADONAI's paths are **grace** and truth to those who keep his covenant and instructions. (CJB)

> All the paths of the LORD are **lovingkindness** and truth to those who keep His covenant and His testimonies. (NASB)

> All the paths of the LORD are **mercy** and truth unto such as keep His covenant and His testimonies. (JPS)

Another Hebrew word for mercy found in the Hebrew Scriptures is *racham*. It is so intimate that its root comes from the relationship of a mother to her unborn child. Most of the time this word, which means compassion, includes "tender" along with "mercy." Abba, the Heavenly Father, is moved by compassionate racham like a mother is for the child who moves in her womb. Adonai is a nurturing Father who gave His children His Torah of life as His instruction manual for how to live a blessed life on the earth.

> Let, I pray thee, thy **merciful kindness** [chesed] be for my comfort, according to thy word unto thy servant. Let thy **tender mercies** [racham] come unto me, that I may live: for thy **law** *is* my delight. (Ps. 119:76-77 KJV)

Too many modern churches teach, "We are under grace," as though grace is opposed to God's law. The "dispensation" of grace is used as an excuse to be disobedient. Should we, as believers in Messiah

Yeshua, continue to sin, now that our hearts have been set free? God forbid. "Now you have been set free from sin, and have become slaves to God. The benefit you reap leads to holiness, and the result is eternal life." (Ro. 6:22 NIV)

In the past, believers in Yeshua were in bondage to sin and its death penalty. Through His lovingkindness [chesed] and mercy [racham], they have been set free to be slaves to righteousness. Through repentance, those who are saved now have a new master that they serve out of wholehearted devotion.

> You are slaves to the one you obey...Thanks be to our God that, though you used to be slaves to sin...You have been set free from sin, and have become slaves to righteousness. (Ro. 6:15-18 NASB)

7

REMEMBER THE TORAH

There is a stirring of the Holy Spirit among God's people to prepare the Way of the LORD. Just as in the time of Yeshua's first coming when John the Baptist came to turn the hearts of the fathers to their children, the Spirit of Elijah is at work today to prepare for Messiah's return.

Malachi Chapter Four tells of the Day of the LORD that is soon coming. It will be a day of destruction for the evildoer, but there are promises for those who fear Adonai, those who remember the commandments of their God.

> But unto you that fear my name shall the Sun of righteousness arise with healing in his wings; and ye shall go forth, and grow up as calves of the stall. (Mal. 4:2 KJV)

> Remember ye the law [Torah instructions] of Moses my servant, which I commanded unto him in Horeb for all Israel, *with* the statutes and judgments. (Mal. 4:3 KJV)

> Behold, I will send you Elijah the
> prophet before the coming of the
> great and dreadful day of the LORD:
> And he shall turn the heart of the
> fathers to the children, and the heart
> of the children to their fathers, lest
> I come and smite the earth with a
> curse. (Mal. 4:5-6 KJV)

These closing passages of the Old Testament, the Hebrew Scriptures, encourage believers to remember the commandments, and which commandment instructs Israel to "remember"?

> Remember the Sabbath day, to
> keep it holy. (Ex. 20:8)

The Sabbath is the engagement ring of the Bride of Messiah; it is a sign upon her hand to remind her to Whom she belongs. Remembering to keep His covenant of mercy is remembering His instructions, and it is an invitation to rest in Him.

Ironically, most churches are big supporters of the words of the prophet Malachi, but it is only in regard to tithing. Pastors and elders hope to prosper their congregations by soliciting charitable contributions, a principle which they substantiate by referring to the prophet Malachi in 3:10. How many sermons have been delivered about being blessed by bringing the "full tithe into God's storehouse"? However, the exhortation is rarely followed by one to heed the rest of God's commandments.

> Malachi's real message is quite
> different than the issue of tithing.
> Malachi is calling God's people
> back to full-bodied endorsement of
> Torah. Malachi's message is about
> how we live, not how we give how
> you give if you aren't obedient to
> His instructions for living? [Malachi]

points out that ignoring God's instructions given to Moses is the equivalent of slapping God in the face. In fact, Malachi mentions (not too subtly) that the day is coming when those who do not live according to the Torah will be swept away in a dreadful day of judgment.. Malachi 3:10 without the rest of the message makes no sense at all. Why would God care about how you give if you aren't obedient to His instructions for living? [Malachi] points out that ignoring God's instructions given to Moses is the equivalent of slapping God in the face. In fact, Malachi mentions (not too subtly) that the day is coming when those who do not live according to the Torah will be swept away in a dreadful day of judgment.

"Remember," says the Lord. The Hebrew verb is *zakar*, but it means a lot more than simple cognition. Remember... Hebrew is an *action* language. So, mental recall will not capture what Malachi commands. To remember is to bring to mind and *act accordingly*. Simply recalling the commandments is not remembering in Hebrew. Remembering means *doing* them! If you don't keep Sabbath, you are not remembering Sabbath. (Moen, 2010)

Abba wants His children to remember His Torah in the last days. Perhaps He chose the word "remember," because He could look into the future and see how His children would forget His Sabbath and need to recall its blessing again.

FREE IN MESSIAH TO OBEY

As a young Jewish boy, it was Yeshua's custom to attend the synagogue on the Sabbath and to hear the Torah and the Prophets. As a grown man, He continued gathering on the Sabbath with the congregation of the righteous to teach Torah and the Prophets. When others suggest another type of Sabbath to keep, either Sunday or a lunar sabbath, defer to the example of Messiah and the apostles who followed Him.

> And Jesus returned in the power of the Spirit into Galilee: and there went out a fame of him through all the region round about. And he taught in their synagogues, being glorified of all. And he came to Nazareth, where he had been brought up: and, as his custom was, he went into the synagogue on the Sabbath day, and stood up for to read. (Lk 4:14-16 KJV)

Messiah's example encourages all His sheep to walk as He did. There is no sin in keeping the Sabbath. It is the way of Messiah and of His people. Honoring the

Sabbath is an identifying mark that one belongs to Yeshua and loves Him.

> And by this we know that we have come to know Him, if we keep His commandments. The one who says, "I have come to know Him," and does not keep His commandments, is a liar, and the truth is not in him; but whoever keeps His word, in him the love of God has truly been perfected. By this we know that we are in Him: the one who says he abides in Him ought himself to walk in the same manner as He walked. (1 Jn 2:3-6 NASB)

Yes, Yeshua objected to some rabbinical interpretations on the observance of the Sabbath day, but not to the *commands* of Torah. Messiah objected to the spirit of legalism that denies the Spirit of the Torah. If one approaches the Sabbath as a way to earn brownie points with God, the goal of Torah is missed. Works of the law were never intended to produce God's favor. Righteous obedience is always driven by a love for Adonai. Honoring Him by joyful service is the goal of Messiah's work in redeemed hearts.

Despite the misconstrued reputation that the Apostle Paul is been given by modern Jewish and Christian scholars, who allege that Paul created a new religion, the truth is that Paul continued his life as a Jew even after coming to faith in Messiah Yeshua. Paul kept the Sabbath as well as the other Biblical feasts of the LORD. There are several references to his being in the synagogue on the Sabbath day. It was also Paul's custom to follow the customs of the Jews.

PAUL AND THE SABBATH

When Paul came to Jerusalem, James and elders met with him to learn of his ministry among the Gentiles. False rumors had circulated among the Jews that Paul was anti-Torah and James came up with a plan to dispel the accusations.

> And when we were come to Jerusalem, the brethren received us gladly. And the *day* following Paul went in with us unto James; and all the elders were present. And when he had saluted them, he declared particularly what things God had wrought among the Gentiles by his ministry. And when they heard *it*, they glorified the Lord, and said unto him, thou see, brother, how many thousands of Jews there are which believe; and they are all zealous of the law: (Acts 21:17-20 KJV)

The first believers were zealous Jews, who loved the Torah, God's law. Paul was being falsely accused of teaching others to forsake the commandments of God. This was NOT true!

> And they [the zealous for Torah,
> Jewish followers of Messiah Yeshua]
> are informed of thee, that thou
> teachest all the Jews which are
> among the Gentiles to forsake
> Moses, saying that they ought not to
> circumcise *their* children, neither to
> walk after the customs [Sabbaths,
> Feast Days, dietary laws, etc.] (Acts
> 21:21 KJV)

James decided to clarify Paul's position, regarding the Torah, by making a public statement. Paul was to go to the Temple with four men, who, along with the Apostle Paul, had previously made a Nazarite vow [3]. This was to be a public demonstration that Paul was in submission to the commands of Torah. Paul made the vow sometime before his arrival in Jerusalem.

> Paul...took leave of the brethren...
> In Cenchrea he had his hair cut, for
> he was keeping a vow. And they
> came to Ephesus, and he left them
> there. Now he himself entered the
> synagogue and reasoned with the
> Jews. (Acts 18:18-19 NASB)

Because of Paul's Nazarite vow, Paul would need to complete the cycle in the Temple and offer the proper sacrifice for the vow. People returning from a long journey, who were unable to travel with rams, ewes, etc. were able to purchase the appropriate animal offering before going into the Temple. Perhaps these were the expenses the four other men had for which Paul paid. James gave the following instructions to Paul.

3. Information on the Nazarite vow is found in Nu. 6:13-21

> Therefore, do this that we tell you.
> We have four men who are under a
> vow; take them and purify yourself
> along with them, and pay their

expenses so that they may shave
their heads; and all will know that
there is nothing to the things which
they have been told about you, but
that you yourself also walk orderly,
keeping the Law. (Acts 21:23-24
NASB)

The Holman Christian Standard Bible describes the
purpose of Paul's instructions given by James and
the elders of Jerusalem was this: "Then everyone will
know that what they were told about you amounts
to nothing, but that you yourself are also careful
about observing the law." (Acts 21:24 CSB)

Paul was attentive to continue to observe the
commandments of God, even after his Damascus
road conversion to faith in Messiah Yeshua. There
are more recent Bible versions that attempt to erase
the Jewishness of the Gospel by excluding or editing
certain passages to fit their paradigm. Acts 18:21 is
one such passage. Compare the Christian Apostle
Paul in the first passage to the Jewish Rabbi *Shaul*
[Paul] in the second.

Paul, having remained many days
longer, took leave of the brethren
and put out to sea for Syria, and
with him were Priscilla and Aquila.
In Cenchrea he had his hair cut,
for he was keeping a vow. They
came to Ephesus, and he left them
there. Now he himself entered the
synagogue and reasoned with the
Jews. When they asked him to stay
for a longer time, he did not consent,
**but taking leave of them and saying,
"I will return to you again if God
wills," he set sail from Ephesus.** (Acts
18:18-21 NASB)

And Paul *after this* tarried *there* yet a

good while, and then took his leave
of the brethren, and sailed thence
into Syria, and with him Priscilla and
Aquila; having shorn *his* head in
Cenchrea: for he had a vow. And
he came to Ephesus, and left them
there: but he himself entered into the
synagogue, and reasoned with the
Jews. When they desired *him* to tarry
longer time with them, he consented
not; But bade them farewell, saying,
I must by all means keep this feast
that cometh in Jerusalem: but I will
return again unto you, if God will.
And he sailed from Ephesus. (Acts
18:18-21 KJV)

Such word choices cause many Christians think
that the Torah, with its Sabbaths associated with
the Feasts of the LORD, had no significance to the
Apostle Paul. Newer Bible versions do not mention
Paul's determination to get to Jerusalem in time
to attend a pilgrimage feast. Why do you suppose
there is this deletion?

The Apostle Shaul was a traveling missionary Rabbi
who attended the synagogues of the cities he visited
to teach about the faith in Messiah Yeshua. The day
that was set aside for teaching was the Sabbath.

Now Paul and his companions...
arrived at Pisidian Antioch, and on
the Sabbath day they went into
the synagogue and sat down. And
after the reading of the Law and
the Prophets the synagogue officials
sent to them, saying, "Brethren, if you
have any word of exhortation for
the people, say it." And Paul stood
up, and motioning with his hand, he
said, "Men of Israel, and you who
fear God, listen: (Acts 13:13-16 NASB)

Those who met Paul and Barnabas in the synagogue of Antioch were impressed by the teaching they received by Rabbi Shaul and begged that he return the following Sabbath to share more.

> And as Paul and Barnabas were going out, the people kept begging that these things might be spoken to them the next Sabbath. Now when *the meeting of* the synagogue had broken up many of the Jews and of the God-fearing proselytes followed Paul and Barnabas, who, speaking to them, were urging them to continue in the grace of God. And the next Sabbath nearly the whole city assembled to hear the word of God. (Acts 13:42 -44 NASB)

Acts 13 tells of Paul being in the synagogue speaking to the men of Israel and to the God-fearing gentiles who worship God. The people, Jew and non-Jew, were blessed by the preaching, and they were encouraged by Paul to continue in the grace of God. Did you catch that? After keeping the Sabbath with the reading and teaching from the Law of God, those who heard were so blessed that they encouraged Paul and Barnabas to continue in the grace of God. There are no New Testament teachings asserting that law and grace are opposing concepts. Even with the controversial Apostle Paul, grace and Torah went hand in hand.

10

THE JERUSALEM ELDERS

The leaders of the Acts 15 Council knew the value of the instructions of Torah that were read each week in the congregations of the righteous. When James spoke up about how to include the God-fearing Gentiles into the synagogues, it was to make it easy for them to access the knowledge of Torah.

> Therefore it is my judgment that we do not trouble those who are turning to God from among the Gentiles, but that we write to them that they abstain from things contaminated by idols and from fornication and from what is strangled and from blood. For Moses from ancient generations has in every city those who preach him, since he is read in the synagogues every Sabbath. (Acts 15:19-21 NASB)

Attitude is everything. When mentioning the reference to Moses, those believing Jews in Jerusalem reverenced the name of Moses. Most modern Christians will speak the name of Moses with disdain, as though the mention of the law and Moses is something disgusting. Before the antinomian[4] theories of the modern church, the elders in Jerusalem decided that the non-Jews were to be welcomed into the synagogues and to share the delight of the Sabbath.

The Torah was to be read each week and the God-fearing Gentiles would learn of Adonai's instructions. As the Spirit led the new converts from among the nations, they would no longer "be conformed to this world, but be transformed" by the renewing of their minds so that they would know what is the good, acceptable and perfect will of God. (Ro. 12:2 NASB)

Growing in grace and wisdom to the first century Apostles was growing in understanding and application of the Torah. It was learning to live life according to the instructions of the divine Creator. It was to form one new man out of the two. The Heavenly Father does not want two houses of worship meeting on two different days of the week. Israel is not in unity when the Jews gather on the Sabbath and the Christians gather on Sunday. In Messiah Yeshua, we are called to be Echad, to be One in Him. When the Torah was given to Israel, there was always a provision of inclusion for God-fearing foreigners to join the congregations of righteous Jews to celebrate the Sabbaths of God.

> One ordinance *shall be both* for you of the congregation, and also for the stranger that sojourns *with you*, an ordinance forever in your generations: as ye *are*, so shall the stranger be before the LORD. One law and one manner shall be for you, and for the stranger that sojourns with you. (Nu. 15:15-16 KJV)

4. The concept that under the "dispensation of grace," the Torah is of no use, as though it has become obsolete.

Messiah Yeshua is the open door for all who believe, be they Jew or non-Jew. He was full of wisdom and grace, kept His Father's commandments, and lived in His love.

On the night Messiah was betrayed, He spoke these words of encouragement to His disciples about continuing in obedience to the commandments of God because of devoted love:

> He who has My commandments and keeps them, it is he who loves Me. And he who loves Me will be loved by My Father, and I will love him and manifest Myself to him. (Jn 14:21 NKJV)

> If you keep My commandments, you will abide in My love, just as I have kept My Father's commandments and abide in His love. (Jn 15:10 NASB)

The apostles of Yeshua continued teaching the traditions of Messiah, including obedience to the commandments of God. Obedience is the mark of loyalty to the King, which the elders in Jerusalem taught and the Apostle Paul continued in.

> By this we know that we love the children of God, when we love God, and keep his commandments. For this is the love of God, that we keep his commandments: and his commandments are not grievous. (1 Jn 5:2-3 KJV)

> And this is love, that we walk after his commandments. This is the commandment, That, as ye have heard from the beginning, ye should walk in it. (2 Jn 1:6 KJV)

Keeping the Sabbath is not a burdensome commandment; it is a delight to enjoy. Sabbath begins on Friday evening at sundown with a sumptuous feast of the best foods, a beautiful table set with candles, fresh-baked challah, and the fruit of the vine, with family gathered around to sing, pray, and give thanks.

Messiah Yeshua is our example to follow. The Elders in Jerusalem and the Apostle Paul also followed the example of his Master. Shouldn't we do the same?

11

I TELL YOU THE TRUTH

The love of the truth is what saves believers from the lies of the enemy. If one loves The Truth and seeks it, one will find it, when it is sought whole-heartedly. Messiah Yeshua is the Way, the Truth, and the Life, and He established the perpetuity of the Torah when He said,

> Do not think that I have come to abolish the Law or the Prophets; I have not come to abolish them but to fulfill them. I tell you the truth, until heaven and earth disappear, not the smallest letter, not the least stroke of a pen, will by any means disappear from the Law until everything is accomplished. (Mt.5:17-18 NIV)

Manipulations of man have attempted, over the past 1700 years, to exchange the sign of covenant from the seventh day Sabbath to the first day of the week. Sunday "Sabbath keeping" is not in accordance with the Truth of the Word of the LORD. In Chapter 14 of this book we will look at Catholic and Protestant confessions about the Sabbath that prove that man has attempted to change God's laws and remove the sign of His covenant with His people.

As believers grow in faith, they are to grow in grace and knowledge of Messiah Yeshua. This gracious gift separates Israel from the world and sanctifies her to Adonai. Honoring commandments honors the King and creates intimacy with Messiah. While the experience of Salvation may feel instantaneous, it is also a process of relationship-building. Just like any marriage, the wedding day is only just the beginning of a new life of being united together as one.

As a disciple grows in the grace and knowledge of Messiah, the mind of the believer is transformed into His image, and one is sanctified, set apart for a holy purpose. Sanctification comes after the initial salvation experience, and it is the work of the Holy Spirit dwelling inside and teaching Messiah's ways so the disciple can walk in His truth.

> Sanctify them in the truth; Thy word is truth. As Thou didst send Me into the world, I also have sent them into the world. And for their sakes I sanctify Myself, that they themselves also may be sanctified in truth. (Jn 17:17-19 NASB)

Choosing to honor the Sabbath and remembering to keep it holy are part of submitting to the Lordship of Messiah. Only the Ruach HaKodesh can convict a person of this and confirm the righteousness of God in the heart. Yielding to His Torah instructions, as the Holy Spirit reveals the Word, is being sanctified in the righteousness of Messiah Yeshua.

The Apostle Paul verifies that sanctification will lead believers to stand firm in the faith and to hold onto the traditions that were taught by the Elders in Jerusalem.

> But we should always give thanks to

> God for you, brethren beloved by
> the Lord, because God has chosen
> you from the beginning for salvation
> through sanctification by the Spirit
> and faith in the truth. And it was
> for this He called you through our
> gospel, that you may gain the glory
> of our Lord Jesus Christ. So then,
> brethren, stand firm and hold to the
> traditions which you were taught,
> whether by word *of mouth* or by
> letter from us. (2 Th. 2:13-15 NASB)

Many times Christians will balk about the need to be sanctified by obedience to the Torah, the Word of God, and some claim that they are "free from the law" because they are New Covenant believers. Is there a "liberty" that allows for disobedience to the commandments of God? The truth is that there is a connection between the Torah and the Spirit. This is the crux of the New Covenant foretold by the prophet Jeremiah.

> "Behold, days are coming," declares
> the LORD, "when I will make a new
> covenant with the house of Israel
> and with the house of Judah, not
> like the covenant which I made
> with their fathers in the day I took
> them by the hand to bring them out
> of the land of Egypt, My covenant
> which they broke, although I was
> a husband to them," declares the
> LORD. "But **this is the covenant**
> which I will make with the house of
> Israel after those days," declares the
> LORD, "**I will put My law within them,
> and on their heart I will write it**; and
> I will be their God, and they shall be
> My people, And they shall not teach
> again, each man his neighbor and
> each man his brother, saying, 'Know

the LORD,' for they shall all know Me, from the least of them to the greatest of them," declares the LORD, "for I will forgive their iniquity, and their sin I will remember no more." (Je. 31:31-34 NASB)

Jeremiah prophesies that instead of doing away with Torah, Adonai will magnify His Torah by writing it on New Covenant hearts. The fault was not with God's Word, His laws, or His commandments. The fault was with His people not receiving His instructions, and therefore, violating their marriage vows. Our Heavenly Bridegroom had to create a way to return His Chosen into covenant keeping status.[5]

> For finding fault with them [ancient Israel, not the commandments], he saith, Behold, the days come, saith the Lord, when I will make a **new covenant** with the house of Israel and with the house of Judah: Not according to the covenant that I made with their fathers in the day when I took them by the hand to lead them out of the land of Egypt; because they continued not in my covenant, and I regarded them not, saith the Lord. For this *is* the covenant that I will make with the house of Israel after those days, saith the Lord; **I will put my laws into their mind, and write them in their hearts**: and I will be to them a God, and they shall be to me a people: And they shall not teach every man his neighbour, and every man his brother, saying, Know the Lord: for all shall know me, from the least to the greatest. For I will be merciful to their unrighteousness, and their sins and their iniquities will I remember no more. (Heb. 8:8-12 KJV)

5. Refer to The Law of the Husband in Chapter 4 of the BEKY Book *Divorce and Remarriage in the Bible* by Robin Gould. D.R.E, LMFT.

The New Covenant, which is commandments kept because of Holy Spirit illumination, also is prophesied by Ezekiel. The connection between Spirit and Torah is highlighted in this restoration of Israel passage in Ezekiel 37.

> I will give you **a new heart** and put **a new spirit** in you; I will remove from you your heart of stone and give you a heart of flesh. And **I will put my Spirit in you and move you to follow my decrees and be careful to keep my laws.** (Ez.36:26 NIV)

Imagine what the world look like if all Christians began to be moved by the power of the Ruach to keep the Torah of God! What if those who profess Messiah Yeshua as Lord and Savior opened their minds to receive the New Covenant written on their hearts? It would be the Kingdom restored on the earth! This is only possible if the children of God choose to yield to the Spirit of Truth that has been sent to be our Helper and to instruct us in the way we should go.

> And I will ask the Father, and He will give you another Helper, that He may be with you forever; *that is* the Spirit of truth, whom the world cannot receive, because it does not behold Him or know Him, *but* you know Him because He abides with you, and will be in you. (Jn 14:16-17 NASB)

Spirit-anointed and led disciples of Messiah Yeshua bear witness of the goodness of God. The engrafted Word, Torah written on the hearts of men, is what the New Covenant is all about.

> When the Helper comes, whom I will send to you from the Father, *that is* the Spirit of truth, who proceeds from

> the Father, He will bear witness of
> Me, and you *will* bear witness also,
> because you have been with Me
> from the beginning. These things I
> have spoken to you that you may
> be kept from stumbling. (Jn 14:16-17,
> 16:1 NASB)

The Spirit and Torah agree. The Ruach leads disciples into all truth. Honoring the Sabbath is one of the jewels of truth that is available to all who call on the name of Messiah.

> But when He, the Spirit of truth,
> comes, He will guide you into all the
> truth; for He will not speak on His own
> initiative, but whatever He hears,
> He will speak; and He will disclose to
> you what is to come. He shall glorify
> Me; for He shall take of Mine, and
> shall disclose *it* to you. All things that
> the Father has are Mine; therefore I
> said, that He takes of Mine, and will
> disclose *it* to you. (Jn 16:13-15 NASB)

In the lawless days in which we live, the Apostle John has these words of encouragement so we can discern truth from error.

> We are from God; he who knows
> God listens to us; he who is not from
> God does not listen to us. By this we
> know the spirit of truth and the spirit
> of error. (1 Jn 4:6 NASB)

The disciples of Yeshua must heed the Master's words; His Word must have the primary role for their lives. His sheep hear His voice if they belong to Him. Pastors need to feed the flock with the Torah of God. False leaders have gone into the world with contrary doctrine, using the Apostle Paul's words to their own destruction. The writings of Paul should be interpreted in light of Messiah. Paul and Messiah are in agreement that the Torah of Adonai is not done away with.

It is a great tragedy that Rabbi Paul and Messiah Yeshua have been so misrepresented by "disciples of Christ" that it is nearly impossible to recognize the Jewishness of the Gospel in most churches today. What would the world experience if all of God's people, Jew and non-Jew, kept the fourth commandment as instructed in the Word of God? What would we experience if the Sabbath was a day of rest all around the world and not in Jerusalem only?

The book of Hebrews reminds New Covenant believers of the need for Shabbat because it remains a sign of His covenant upon our hearts. "There remains therefore a Sabbath rest for the people of God." (Heb. 4:9 NASB)

King David, after his return to righteousness, was completely in love with God's Torah. Psalms 119 is full of his devotion to the truth of God's eternal Word. "Thy righteousness *is* an everlasting righteousness, and thy law *is* the truth." (Ps.119:142)

12

DELIGHT IN YOUR COMMANDS

The charge may now arise that those who keep the Sabbath are being legalistic. If you ask if we love the Torah, our answer is "yes." Do we judge others' salvation experience on works of the law? The answer is "no". Torah has no power to save, but to convict of sin. Torah *does* have the authority to demonstrate to a redeemed people how to live a life pleasing to God while on the earth. The Psalms are full of praises for the Torah, the instructions for right living according to the Word of Adonai.

> **Blessed** *is* the man that walketh not in the counsel of the ungodly, nor standeth in the way of sinners, nor sitteth in the seat of the scornful. But **his delight *is* in the law** of the LORD; and in his law doth he meditate day and night. (Ps 1:1-2 KJV)

> I will walk about in freedom, for I have sought out your precepts...for I **delight in your commands** because I love them. (Ps 119:44-48 NIV)

> **I delight to do thy will**, O my God:

yea, **thy law *is* within my heart**...
Withhold not thou thy tender
mercies from me, O LORD: let
thy lovingkindness and thy truth
continually preserve me. (Ps. 40:8-11
KJV)

Doing your will, my God, is my joy;
your *Torah* is in my inmost being. (Ps.
40:9 CJB)

Blessed *are* the undefiled in the
way, **who walk in the law of the
LORD.** Blessed *are* they that keep his
testimonies, *and that* seek him with
the whole heart. (Ps.119:1-2 KJV)

Give me understanding, and I shall
keep thy law; yea, I shall observe it
with *my* whole heart. Make me to go
in the path of thy commandments;
for therein do I delight. (Ps. 119:34-35
KJV)

I have longed for thy salvation
[Yeshua], O LORD; and **thy law
[Torah] *is* my delight**. (Ps. 119:174
KJV)

Torah is not necessary for salvation, "For it is by grace
you have been saved and not by works" (Ep 2:8).
Salvation depends on the grace given through faith
in Messiah Yeshua. One can never earn righteousness
through doing the right things. It is the LORD alone
who is righteous, and He imparts that righteousness
to believers through faith in Messiah Yeshua. Once
we have entered the New Covenant, the Torah is
written on our hearts and minds. It is not done away
with, but it is inside of each believer. It is who we are,
as followers of Messiah.

As a believer grows in knowledge of Messiah, he

or she becomes conformed to the image of Him. The disciple becomes more like Yeshua as the Holy Spirit moves him or her to follow His commands. The observance of Torah has nothing to do with salvation, but everything to do with sanctification. Sin is violation of God's Torah (1 Jn 3:4). Once a person is redeemed, he should make every effort to resist sin and not to grieve the Holy Spirit. To continue in Torah violations is not the mark of a disciple of Messiah.

The Scriptures are given for correction, instruction, and training in righteousness. We must give our ears to the full counsel of His Word contained from Genesis to Revelation. Believers need to give their hearts to understanding, to seek out His ways that are higher than human ways. A lover of Yeshua should boldly walk along the road less traveled and to find the narrow way that leads to Him. Our testimony should be that of our Messiah, "The prince of this world has no hold on me, but the world must learn that I love the Father and that I do exactly what my Father has commanded me." (Jn 14:30-31)

13

OBSERVING SHABBAT

For those who are first considering observing the Sabbath, it is important not burden one's self with being "correct" about honoring the day. Don't look for the prescription of how to do everything right according to man's interpretation for the day. Yes, while rabbinic Judaism has come down with a large list for what is permissible and what is not permissible for the Sabbath, it would be cumbersome for a newcomer to sort through it all and find peace. Shabbat is all about Shalom, which is the peace that comes from God. Growing in understanding and knowledge about the Sabbath takes years of time, so set the pace accordingly.

Begin by recognizing the day as distinct from all the other days of the week. Set it apart as holy, and choose to focus on what draws you closer to the Creator. It is an opportunity to get rid of the distractions of a frenetic lifestyle and slow down the pace. Demanding schedules and running to and fro are not part of Shabbat. Chaos and worldly concerns are not part of Shabbat. Struggles and strivings with man are not part of Shabbat. Whatever was of concern in the worldly arena of life is to be set aside for twenty-four hours.

Sabbath is not a time to work on spouses or children. It is not a time to change friends' opinions or instruct them in what we think they should be doing. Shabbat is a day to give everyone a break from our expectations and just enjoy their presence. It is not a time to try to change people by counsel or intervention. It is a time to let go and let God. Creating ceases in order to give life a rest.

Shabbat is a time to commune, defined as talking together with profound intensity of thoughts and feelings, with Adonai and His children about His Word. It is precious time to listen, really listen, to His Instructions.

Friday night is filled with expectancy because it is a weekly date night with the King of the Universe. Anticipate that He will reveal intimate things about one's personal walk on the journey to Zion. Especially on Friday night, and into the morning of Shabbat, He may give one significant dreams and revelation about where the Spirit is leading.

For observance in the home, families create a peaceful environment for the weekly Shabbat dinner meal on Friday night. A thorough house cleaning on Friday morning sets the tone that this day is special. It is as though special dignitaries are arriving at the family door at sunset Friday night, and they are! The family prepares as if Yeshua is coming to sit and dine at the table, because He is!

It heightens anticipation to freshen up and put on one's best clothes as if we are going out to a fine dining establishment. Beautiful background worship music that soothes the soul after a hectic week is wonderful for the family to come home to.

A few simple signs of Shabbat can be introduced into the Friday night meal, such as *challah*, two freshly baked loaves of bread, one for Friday night and the other for Saturday. Grape juice or wine is included for the blessings. Two candles flickering on the dining table, along with a delicious meal, including dessert, can help set the day apart.

CANDLE LIGHTING

To distinguish the Sabbath from all the other days of the week, the woman of the home is given the honor to initiate the Shabbat by lighting two candles. All the feasts of the LORD are initiated by women illuminating the darkness with a blessing. This act is a representation of welcoming the Shekinah presence of the Holy Spirit into the home. There are beautiful hand motions and spiritually uplifting movements may be made when the words are uttered, but they are not commanded in Scripture. They are traditions that validate setting apart the time of Sabbath as sacred. The blessing spoken over the lighting of the candles in Messianic Jewish homes is:

> Blessed are you O Lord our God, King of the Universe, Who has sanctified us in Your Word, and given us Yeshua our Messiah, and commanded us to be light to the world. Amen.[6]

KIDDUSH - BLESSING OVER THE WINE AND BREAD

Included in the Sabbath meal blessings over the wine and bread are simple recognized symbols of Communion. The blessing spoken over the wine or grape juice is called *Kiddush*, and it means sanctification. Speaking this blessing separates the work week from the day of rest:

> The Sixth Day. The heavens and the earth were completed in all their array. And on the seventh day, God finished the work He had done, and He rested on the seventh day from all the work He had done. And God blessed the seventh day and made

6. Greenberg, 2014

65

it holy, because He rested on it from all His work that God created to do.

> Blessed are You, O Lord our God,
> King of the Universe, Who created
> the fruit of the vine.[7]

Remember the connection to Passover with these words. Yeshua is the vine, and we are the branches. It is in Him that believers live and move and have their being. It is through His blood that Israel is saved, and the Sabbath wine is a symbol of what was poured out to redeem His people.

The blessing for the bread is:

> Blessed are You, O Lord our God,
> King of the Universe, Who brings forth
> bread from the Earth.

Yeshua is the Bread of Life. He came forth and was raised out of the earthen tomb at His First Fruits resurrection. This blessing has an added benefit of a reminder of the power of the Holy Spirit to bring life from the dead, a Messianic hope that the weekly Sabbath reminds believers to speak about.

As the family grows in keeping the Sabbath, the blessings over the bread and wine can be learned in Hebrew as well. It is good to know that the Hebrew blessings over the bread are the very words Messiah Yeshua spoke when He lifted up bread and gave thanks. These words are ancient connections to an eternal blessing.

Other traditions that support the family structure around the Shabbat table are the blessings for the Woman of Valor from Proverbs 31. This is a blessing that a husband addresses to his wife:

7. Greenberg, 2014

- A woman of valour who can find? for her price is far above rubies. The

heart of her husband doth safely trust
in her, and he hath no lack of gain.

- She doeth him good and not
evil all the days of her life.

- She seeketh wool and flax, and
worketh willingly with her hands.

- She is like the merchant-ships; she
bringeth her food from afar.

- She riseth also while it is yet night,
and giveth food to her household,
and a portion to her maidens.

- She considereth a field, and
buyeth it; with the fruit of her hands
she planteth a vineyard.

- She girdeth her loins with strength,
and maketh strong her arms.

- She perceiveth that her merchandise is
good; her lamp goeth not out by night.

- She layeth her hands to the distaff,
and her hands hold the spindle.

- She stretcheth out her hand to
the poor; yea, she reacheth forth
her hands to the needy.

- She is not afraid of the snow for her
household; for all her household
are clothed with scarlet.

- She maketh for herself coverlets; her
clothing is fine linen and purple.

- Her husband is known in the gates, when
he sitteth among the elders of the land.

- She maketh linen garments and
  selleth them; and delivereth
  girdles unto the merchant.

- Strength and dignity are her clothing;
  and she laugheth at the time to come.

- She openeth her mouth with wisdom; and
  the law of kindness is on her tongue.

- She looketh well to the ways
  of her household, and eateth
  not the bread of idleness.

- Her children rise up, and call her blessed;
  her husband also, and he praiseth her:

- 'Many daughters have done valiantly,
  but thou excellest them all.'

- Grace is deceitful, and beauty is
  vain; but a woman that feareth
  the LORD, she shall be praised.

- Give her of the fruit of her hands;
  and let her works praise her in
  the gates. (Pr. 31:10-31 JPS)

The Proverbs 31 Woman is a parable of the Holy Spirit, who infills all Believers in Messiah Yeshua. This is the Bride the King is instructed to search for.

The husband may be blessed in return by his wife with Psalms 1:1-3 spoken over him.

> How blessed are those who reject
> the advice of the wicked, don't
> stand on the way of sinners or sit
> where scoffers sit!
>
> Their delight is in ADONAI's *Torah*;
> on his *Torah* they meditate day and

night.

> They are like trees planted by
> streams - they bear their fruit in
> season, their leaves never wither,
> everything they do succeeds. (CJB)

Then the children, gathered around the Sabbath table, are blessed by the laying on of hands or by being covered under their father's tallit (prayer shawl).

> May God make you like Ephraim
> and Manasseh.

> May God make you like Sarah and
> Rebecca, Rachel, and Leah.

The following blessing is from the Aaronic Benediction, and it is spoken over everyone.

> May Yahweh bless you and keep
> you;

> May Yahweh make His face to shine
> upon you and be gracious to you;

> May Yahweh lift up His countenance
> upon you and give you peace.

While the beauty of a prayerful home-centered entrance into Shabbat is extremely spiritually uplifting, and even adding music and the reading of the weekly Torah portions is illuminating, Shabbat is not Shabbat without a holy convocation. Scripture commands Israel to gather with the redeemed community for edification, teaching, worship, and service to one another. God intended for His people to congregate on the Sabbath. It is His day to direct His children, individually at home and corporately as well, when we gather on His Sabbath.

> Six days shall work be done: but the
> seventh day *is* the Sabbath of rest,
> a holy convocation; ye shall do no
> work *therein*: it *is* the Sabbath of the
> LORD in all your dwellings. (Le. 23:3
> KJV)

Some Hebraic Roots congregations resemble a contemporary church service in their style of worship when they gather on the Sabbath. Others adopt a synagogue pattern of worship. Both are good, because both help connect people to the unity of the faith that Messiah Yeshua desires. For more information, about what one may experience when attending a Messianic Sabbath service, please read the BEKY Book, *Messianic Shabbat Service*, by Dr. Hollisa Alewine.

14

PROTESTANT AND CATHOLIC CONFESSIONS

Throughout history there has been a faithful remnant of followers of Messiah Yeshua who have upheld the commandments of God and kept His testimony. It is a most persecuted group, but their witness as overcomers is powerful. Religious leaders have attempted to blot out their record and silence them. In Christianity there is a dark history of anti-Semitism and suppression of the truth of God's Word. Both the Catholic and Protestant leaders are guilty of these crimes, and their own words reveal their misalignment with the Author and Finisher of the faith.

In September of 1893, the *Catholic Mirror* was published under the authority of James Cardinal Gibbons with the following statements regarding the Sabbath and the Protestant Christian conformance to the authority of the Pope, who established Sunday as the New Testament "Sabbath":

> Thus, it is impossible to find in
> the New Testament the slightest
> interference by the Saviour or his
> Apostles with the original Sabbath...

for thirty years after His death, as the Acts of the Apostles has abundantly testified...Hence the conclusion is inevitable...that of those who follow the Bible as their guide, the Israelites and Seventh-day Adventists have exclusive weight of evidence on their side, whilst the Biblical Protestant has not a word in self-defense for his substitution of Sunday for Saturday[8].

Having proved to a demonstration that the Redeemer, *in no instance*, had, during the period of His life, deviated from the faithful observance of the Sabbath (Saturday), referred to by the four evangelists fifty-one times, although He had designated Himself "Lord of the Sabbath," He never having *once*, by command or practice, hinted at a desire on His part to change the day by the substitution of another...[9]

In the above pamphlet, references are made to the sixty-one times the validity of the Sabbath is mentioned in the New Testament verses and the eight times the first day of the week is mentioned. The author continues with a slam against all Protestants who think they are following "only Scripture" for the basis of their Sabbath worship and the "authority" of the Catholic church to change God's perpetual Shabbat covenant decree.

8. Gibbons, 1893, pg. 8

9. Ibid

What Protestant can, after perusing these articles, with a clear conscience, continue to disobey the command of God, enjoining Saturday to be kept, which command his teacher, the Bible, from Genesis to Revelation, records as the will of God?[10]

The first proposition needs little proof. The Catholic Church for over one thousand years before the existence of a Protestant, by virtue of her divine mission, changed the day from Saturday to Sunday.[11]

There is not one Scripture to verify that the Sabbath was changed from the last day of the week to the first. It is the vain traditions of man that have been handed down through the generations, causing sincere Christians to observe days that were never sanctioned by God as the Sabbath. It is time the Protestant Reformation continues to reform believers away from the traditions of man in favor of the Torah of Adonai.

The following are Catholic and Protestant confessions about the Sabbath.[12]

ROMAN CATHOLIC CONFESSIONS

James Cardinal Gibbons, *The Faith of our Fathers*, 88th ed., pp. 89.

"But you may read the Bible from Genesis to Revelation, and you will not find a single line authorizing the sanctification of Sunday. The Scriptures enforce the religious observance of Saturday, a day which we never sanctify."

Stephen Keenan, *A Doctrinal Catechism* 3rd ed., p. 174.

"Question: Have you any other way of proving that the Church

10. *The Catholic Mirror*, published Sept. 23, 1883

11. Ibid

12. "Roman Catholic and Protestant Confessions about Sunday" - Bible Sabbath Association

has power to institute festivals of precept?

"Answer: Had she not such power, she could not have done that in which all modern religionists agree with her-she could not have substituted the observance of Sunday, the first day of the week, for the observance of Saturday, the seventh day, a change for which there is no Scriptural authority."

PROTESTANT CONFESSIONS

Isaac Williams, *Plain Sermons on the Catechism*, vol. 1, pp.334, 336.

"And where are we told in the Scriptures that we are to keep the first day at all? We are commanded to keep the seventh; but we are nowhere commanded to keep the first day...The reason why we keep the first day of the week holy instead of the seventh is for the same reason that we observe many other things, not because the Bible, but because the church has enjoined it."

Canon Eyton, *The Ten Commandments*, pp. 52, 63, 65.

"There is no word, no hint, in the New Testament about abstaining from work on Sunday....into the rest of Sunday no divine law enters... The observance of Ash Wednesday or Lent stands exactly on the same footing as the observance of Sunday."

Bishop Seymour, *Why We Keep Sunday*.

"We have made the change from the seventh day to the first day, from Saturday to Sunday, on the authority of the one holy Catholic Church."

Dr. Edward T. Hiscox, a paper read before a New York ministers' conference, Nov. 13, 1893, reported in *New York Examiner*, Nov.16, 1893.

"There was and is a commandment to keep holy the Sabbath day, but that Sabbath day was not Sunday. It will be said, however, and with some show of triumph, that the Sabbath was transferred from the seventh to the first day of the week...Where can the record of such a transaction be found? Not in the New Testament, absolutely not."

"To me it seems unaccountable that Jesus, during three years' intercourse with His disciples, often conversing with them upon the Sabbath question...never alluded to any transference of the day; also, that during forty days of His resurrection life, no such thing was intimated."

"Of course, I quite well know that Sunday did come into use in early Christian history...But what a pity it comes branded with the mark of paganism, and christened with the name of the sun god, adopted and sanctioned by the papal apostasy, and bequeathed as a sacred legacy to Protestantism!"

John Theodore Mueller, Sabbath or Sunday, pp. 15, 16.

"But they err in teaching that Sunday has taken the place of the Old Testament Sabbath and therefore must be kept as the seventh day had to be kept by the children of Israel .... These churches err in their teaching, for Scripture has in no way ordained the first day of the week in place of the Sabbath. There is simply no law in the New Testament to that effect."

T. C. Blake, D.D., Theology Condensed, pp.474, 475.

"The Sabbath is a part of the decalogue - the Ten Commandments. This alone forever settles the question as to the perpetuity of the institution... Until, therefore, it can be shown that the whole moral law has been repealed, the Sabbath will stand... The teaching of Christ confirms the perpetuity of the Sabbath."

D. L. Moody, Weighed and Wanting (Fleming H. Revell Co.: New York), pp. 47, 48.

"The Sabbath was binding in Eden, and it has been in force ever since. This fourth commandment begins with the word 'remember,' showing that the Sabbath already existed when God wrote the law on the tables of stone at Sinai. How can men claim that this one commandment has been done

away with when they will admit that
the other nine are still binding?"

15

REPENTANCE

Good LORD willing, the information contained in this booklet has caused careful consideration of God's perpetual commandment regarding His Day of Delight, the Sabbath. If this material is new, it may disrupt one's spiritual world view, yet the foundation of our faith in the Word is solid. For our faith is in Messiah Yeshua and His finished work. His disciples are to follow Him and walk as He walked.

Traditions of man have been handed down through the generations, and they are deeply ingrained into our culture. Sometimes in order to change, to align one's self with the instructions of Messiah, it requires a 180° turn around. In Hebrew, repentance is called *teshuva*, and it implies turning from ungodliness and returning to the ways of Adonai. Sometimes the Heavenly Father has to shake us to wake us. If this has shaken you, it is time to awaken!

> Awake, awake, clothe yourself in
> your strength, O Zion; clothe yourself
> in your beautiful garments, O
> Jerusalem, the holy city; (Is. 51:1)

If the conviction of the Holy Spirit is upon you, it is

a good day to repent. Ask Messiah Yeshua to be Lord of your life, and for His Holy Spirit to lead you in how you are to walk out your faith. Ask the LORD, Yahweh, to forgive you of everything the Bible calls sin and cleanse you of all iniquity. Turn to Him with whole-hearted devotion, by being willing to follow His Word and walk in His ways. The joy you will feel from the release of religious bondage will strengthen you on the way to Zion.

Shabbat Shalom!

QUESTIONS FOR REVIEW

1. How does honoring the Sabbath proclaim Whom you belong to?

2. Why is the Sabbath a sign of God's Covenantal faithfulness?

3. Who is called to keep the Sabbath and take hold of Adonai's covenant?

4. Can man change what has been declared holy by God?

5. How is chesed (lovingkindness) and racham (tender mercy) part of God's expression of His covenant with Israel?

6. According to Acts 21:17-20, what was the attitude of the first century believers towards the Torah?

7. In light of Hebrews 8:8-12 and Jeremiah 31:31-34, with whom is the New Covenant made?

8. According to Scripture, what does whole-hearted devotion to Adonai look like?

9. With a full heart of Torah, how are believers in Messiah set free?

10. Considering the Catholic and Protestant confessions on the Sabbath, how does this shatter the illusion of godliness that the traditions of man have handed down?

REFERENCES

"Am Segulah - The Biblical Status of the Bride." (2009, February 14). kolsimcha.org. Retrieved 12/30/16 from <http://www.kolsimcha.org/messages/2009/021409M.pdf>.

Gibbons, J. (Ed). (1893, September 23). *The Catholic Mirror*.

Greenburg, J. (2014). *Messianic Shabbat siddur*. Tampa: Messianic Liturgical Resources.

Moen, Skip. (2015, August 15). *Hebrew Word Study* Retrieved 1/5/17 from <https://skipmoen.com/2015/08/gods-grandchildren/>.

_____. (2010, January 24). *Hebrew Word Study*. Retrieved 1/6/17 from <https://skipmoen.com/2010/01/prophetic-profits/>.

"Roman Catholic and Protestant Confessions about Sunday." Bible Sabbath Association. Retrieved 1/6/17 from http://www.biblesabbath.org/confessions.html

Sacks, J. (2008). *The Koren Yom Kippur Mahzor - Nasah Ashkenaz*. Jerusalem: Koren Publishers.

ABOUT THE AUTHOR

For the past thirty years, Jane Diffenderfer has been a devoted mother to nine children, seven sons and two daughters, all of whom were home educated. Jane has experience on the front lines and in the trenches in the Messianic, Hebraic Roots movement, as a ministry leader and pastor for over twenty years. She has a passion for women and for teaching them who they are in Messiah Yeshua. In 2012, Jane founded Women of Valor ministry to encourage female  image bearers and co-laborers in the Kingdom of God, in an equal and counter balanced partnership with their brothers in Messiah Yeshua.

91237896R00051

Made in the USA
Lexington, KY
19 June 2018